I0838000

THE LOVERS OF LUXURY

Passion and Prejudice

Edimilson Franca

CONTENTS

Title Page

Introduction ... 3

Chapter 1: Between Diamonds and Doubts ... 6

Chapter 2: The Look of Nonconformity ... 11

Chapter 3: Echoes of a Decision ... 16

Chapter 4: Secrets of a Past ... 21

Chapter 5: The Game of Appearances ... 26

Chapter 6: Between Luxury and Truth ... 31

Chapter 7: Secrets Revealed ... 35

Chapter 8: The Price of Truth ... 40

Chapter 9: Broken Ties ... 44

Chapter 10: Shadows of the Past ... 48

Chapter 11: Encounters and Mismatches ... 53

Chapter 12: The Price of Truth ... 58

Chapter 13: Shadows of the Past ... 63

Chapter 14: Echoes of Fate ... 67

Chapter 15: The Game of Truth ... 72

Chapter 16: The Refuge of Truth ... 77

Chapter 17: The Revelation of the Past ... 81

Chapter 18: The Challenge of Truth ... 86

Chapter 19: The Return to Normality ... 90

The Lovers of Luxury: Passion and Prejudice

INTRODUCTION

Amid the blinding glare of a city where luxury and ostentation dictate the rules, a love story emerges that defies convention and exposes the frailties of human hearts. **"The Lovers of Luxury: Passion and Prejudice"** it is more than a novel; is a deep immersion into a world of wealth and glamour, where true love is put to the test by social barriers and deep-rooted prejudices.

At first glance, the protagonists' lives may seem like a modern fairy tale, filled with majestic mansions, gala events and a never-ending parade of jewelry and haute couture clothes. However, behind the superficial gloss lie deep challenges and emotional conflicts that shape the true heart of the narrative.

Get to know **Isabella Montgomery**, a young and elegant heiress to the immense Montgomery family fortune, whose parents are known for their influence in the highest spheres of society. Isabella lives a life that many would consider ideal: her routine is filled with sophisticated social events, international travel and the comfort of a stunning mansion. However, behind her radiant smiles and impeccable appearances, Isabella carries a feeling of confinement, a longing for something more genuine and true that the superficiality of high society cannot offer.

On the other side of the city, in a diametrically opposite environment, is **Lucas Ferreira**, a young entrepreneur of modest descent, whose ambition and talent led him to accumulate significant wealth. Lucas grew up in a humble neighborhood, where dreams of greatness were often overshadowed by harsh reality. His journey is marked by an impressive rise, but also by a constant effort to prove his worth in a world that often sees him as an outsider. For Lucas, the luxury and wealth he has achieved are a reward for the challenges he has overcome, but he also faces the constant weight of expectations and prejudice that accompanies his success.

Their fates intersect at a luxurious gala event, a setting that encapsulates the duality of their lives. The first exchange of glances between Isabella and Lucas is filled with palpable tension, a mix of curiosity and resistance. Isabella, accustomed to admirers who court her out of interest, finds in Lucas an authenticity that attracts her and, at the same time, challenges her. Lucas, in turn, is captivated by Isabella's beauty and grace, but is also confronted with the reality that his humble origins place him in a disadvantageous position in a world where status is everything.

As the story unfolds, the connection between Isabella and Lucas deepens, revealing a passion that defies all convention. However, their relationship is constantly threatened by social barriers and deep prejudices. The difference between their origins and the expectations imposed by their respective social spheres creates an emotional battlefield that tests the solidity of their feelings and the resilience of their hearts.

The challenges they face are not just limited to external criticism. Isabella and Lucas are also forced to confront their own fears and insecurities. Isabella must deal with her family's expectations and the judgmental eyes of high society, while Lucas faces the dilemma of balancing his personal aspirations with his desire to be accepted in a world that views him with disdain.

In the midst of this, the luxury that initially seemed like a promise of happiness turns out to be a trap of superficiality and disillusionment.

"The Lovers of Luxury: Passion and Prejudice" explores, with depth and nuance, how true love can flourish in an environment marked by ostentation and prejudice. The narrative reveals how the protagonists challenge established norms and fight for a relationship that transcends class and status barriers. It's a story about the search for authenticity in a world that often privileges appearances and conformity.

In this novel, each chapter is a piece of an emotional puzzle that reveals the highs and lows of a forbidden and intense love story. Isabella and Lucas aren't just characters in a luxury fantasy; they are reflections of a universal desire for true connection and acceptance. **"The Lovers of Luxury: Passion and Prejudice"** is a celebration of passion and perseverance, an ode to the power of love to overcome prejudice and transform lives. In a world where the shine of luxury can overshadow people's true worth, this story shines as a testament to the strength of love and the ability of human beings to transcend their circumstances and find true happiness.

CHAPTER 1: BETWEEN DIAMONDS AND DOUBTS

It was a cold, starry night in New York City, and the opulence of a gala event was in full effect. The lights from the crystal chandeliers illuminated the room to transform the room into a sea of gold and silver. The grandeur of the event was not only a reflection of the wealth of the hosts, but also a stage where the highest spheres of society met to celebrate the magnificence of their lives. The soft sound of the orchestra filled the air, while the scent of rare flowers and expensive perfumes mingled with the aroma of the gourmet delicacies served.

Isabella Montgomery, the young heiress of New York's most influential clan, entered the ballroom with the grace and confidence that only money and an elitist education can provide. Her evening gown, a dazzle of silk and gold embroidery, accentuated her beauty and elegance. Accompanied by her father, Henry Montgomery, a business magnate known for his influence in the financial sector, Isabella seemed to be the embodiment of social perfection.

However, behind the impeccable facade, Isabella felt a whirlwind of conflicting emotions. She was used to being the center of attention, but tonight, something felt different. The glamor of the event, although dazzling, could not mask the sense of boredom and lack of purpose she felt. Isabella wondered if her life, full of luxury and appearances, really had meaning, or if everything was just a performance meticulously rehearsed for the public.

Meanwhile, Lucas Ferreira was on his way to the same event, although his presence there was the result of a series of coincidences and strategic decisions. Lucas, a young entrepreneur who made his fortune in the technology sector, had been invited as a gesture of recognition for his recent philanthropic contribution. The opportunity to attend the event was both recognition and a chance to make important contacts, but Lucas couldn't deny the discomfort he felt entering this world so different from his own.

His suit, although couture, seemed out of place among the extravagantly sophisticated outfits that dominated the room. The difference wasn't just in the clothing, but in the palpable feeling that he didn't belong there. Lucas was aware that despite his success, he was still seen by many as an outsider, an uncomfortable reminder that success could come from unexpected places.

The first exchange of glances between Isabella and Lucas was almost imperceptible to the other guests, but for both of them, it was a moment full of meaning. Isabella was in the middle of a boring conversation with a group of socialites when her eyes met Lucas's. The intensity and authenticity she saw in him was a stark contrast to the superficiality of others present. Lucas, in turn, was immediately captivated by Isabella's beauty and presence, but he also felt intimidated by her aura of perfection and the world she represented.

Fate, always capricious, meant that Isabella and Lucas met again around the buffet. Lucas was trying to familiarize himself with the event's delicacies, while Isabella was looking for something to distract her from her feeling of confinement. A casual conversation began, and although both tried to maintain an appearance of cordiality and interest, there was an underlying tension that was far from merely social.

Isabella, with her refined manners, asked a question about Lucas' interests, and he, in turn, responded with a mixture of sincerity and a hint of humility. The initial dialogue was marked by genuine curiosity and an implicit need to escape the conventions that governed that environment.

As they talked, Isabella discovered that Lucas had grown up in a modest neighborhood and that his rise to success had been marked by hard work and resilience. Lucas, on the other hand, was impressed by Isabella's intelligence and charisma, which seemed to challenge the stereotypical image of the rich, uninteresting socialite.

The conversation flowed naturally, and both began to share their views on life, their ambitions and their frustrations. For Isabella, Lucas represented an escape from the monotonies of her world, a different perspective that offered a refreshing view of life. To Lucas, Isabella was a fascinating enigma, a window into a world of luxury he had conquered but never fully understood.

The night wore on, and although Isabella and Lucas tried to keep a low profile, there was something undeniable about the connection that had formed between them. They were both aware that their conversations were beginning to stray from the casual topic and delve into more personal matters. The enchantment was growing, but there was also a sense that something bigger was at play.

However, the reality of the situation set in when Henry Montgomery, Isabella's father, approached. The formal introduction between Lucas and Henry was courteous, but the difference in status between the two was palpable. Henry, with his calculating gaze and imposing posture, treated Lucas with a cordiality that hid an undertone of disdain. For Henry, Lucas was a reminder of sudden upward mobility and the vulnerability it represented.

As the event drew to a close, Isabella and Lucas were forced to separate, with a sense of uncertainty hanging in the air. The farewell was brief, but full of unspoken promises and a feeling that this meeting was just the beginning of something bigger.

Isabella returned to her home in a luxurious limousine, but her mind was far from the charms of the night. She thought about Lucas, about his authenticity and the way he had broken the monotony of her life. She felt confused about what this meeting meant and how she should deal with the growing feeling that there was something more outside the walls of her golden mansion.

Lucas, in turn, returned to his modern apartment, but the glow of the city and the night lights failed to dispel the restlessness he felt. He wondered if there was any future to the connection he had experienced with Isabella and how he could reconcile this new feeling with the expectations and reality of his own world.

"Between Diamonds and Doubts" marks the beginning of a complex and emotional journey, where true love will be tested by the barriers of social status, prejudice and self-image. As Isabella and Lucas find themselves increasingly involved with each other, they will face not only the external challenges posed by their different backgrounds, but also the internal doubts that threaten to dismantle the fragile bond they are beginning to build. The path ahead is filled with promise and setbacks, and the true test will be their ability to navigate these turbulent waters in search of a love that transcends the limitations imposed by their distinct realities.

CHAPTER 2: THE LOOK OF NONCONFORMITY

The day after the gala event brought with it a new wave of challenges and reflections for Isabella Montgomery and Lucas Ferreira. As the city resumed its frenetic pace, each of the protagonists began to process the profound impact of the encounter they had had the night before.

Isabella woke up with a feeling of restlessness that continued throughout her morning. His morning routine, normally marked by calculated charm and an absolute command over his responsibilities, now seemed strangely empty. Breakfast in the large kitchen of his mansion, filled with fine china and exquisite delicacies, did not offer the same satisfaction as before. Her thoughts were fixed on Lucas, on the conversations they had shared and on the sensations he had awakened in her.

What disturbed her most was the way Lucas had challenged her perceptions. Amid all the protocols and formalities that used to fill his life, Lucas seemed to be a breath of fresh air. Her authenticity and sincerity had created such a sharp contrast to the superficiality that usually surrounded her. Isabella felt a growing need to understand what made Lucas stand out so vividly in her mind and how that feeling fit into her carefully structured life.

She found herself questioning what she really wanted for the future. The luxury and wealth that had always been the basis of his life now seemed like a mere backdrop to a deeper search for meaning and connection. Her mind went back to her conversations with Lucas, his expressive eyes, and the way he spoke with genuine passion about his own challenges and achievements. These memories were accompanied by a persistent doubt: could true love really blossom amidst so much superficiality?

Across town, Lucas was also struggling to make sense of the night before. He woke up in his modern apartment, surrounded by stylish furniture and cutting-edge technology, but the sense of accomplishment seemed to slip through his fingers. He had achieved something that many of his fellow businessmen envied, but at the same time, he had found a new layer of complexity in his encounter with Isabella.

Lucas knew that his rise to wealth had been marked by hard work and sacrifice, but he was unprepared for the way that meeting Isabella had challenged his vision of success and happiness. The authenticity he found in her seemed to be the missing piece in his life, a stark contrast to the often cold and calculating world he had found himself in. He wondered if it was possible to build a real connection in an environment that often valued status and appearance more than an individual's true substance.

Lucas's morning was filled with a similar routine as usual, but the thought of Isabella wouldn't leave him alone. His thoughts wandered through the details of the previous night, trying to decipher what it meant to him and how he could take that feeling forward. There was a growing feeling that he needed to act, but he wasn't sure how.

Fate again made their paths cross, this time at a less formal event, an art exhibition at a local gallery. Isabella had been invited to participate to support an artist friend, and Lucas, in turn, was also present to explore new investment opportunities. Both were aware of the possibility of meeting again, and the expectation of a new interaction was somewhat disconcerting for both.

Isabella arrived at the gallery with her usual elegance, but there was a lightness in her step that seemed to reflect a desire to free herself from the shackles of her usual social life. She was determined to see the works on display, but her mind was on the possibility of meeting Lucas. There was something about his presence that made Isabella feel like there was something more to explore, something that could bring a new perspective to her life.

Lucas arrived at the gallery and was immediately drawn to the vibrant atmosphere and artworks that defied conventionality. The gallery was filled with notable figures and art enthusiasts, but Lucas felt most focused on one specific figure: Isabella. He spotted her across the room, intently examining a modern painting, with a gaze that seemed to reflect both curiosity and introspection.

As he approached Isabella, Lucas was overcome by a mixture of excitement and apprehension. The initial interaction was marked by a cordial greeting and a casual comment about the art they were observing. Yet the tension between them was palpable, a mix of curiosity and a desire to explore something they both knew was more meaningful than a simple exchange of words.

Isabella and Lucas talked about the art on display, but soon the conversation turned to more personal issues. They began to share thoughts and feelings about what they had experienced since their last meeting. The conversation flowed naturally, and they both began to open up in ways they hadn't before.

For Isabella, the conversation with Lucas at the gallery was an opportunity to explore her own doubts and frustrations about the life she had built. She talked about feeling trapped in an existence marked by expectations and conventions, and how this had begun to affect her vision of the future. Lucas, in turn, spoke about his own challenges, his ambitions and the difficulty of finding a real connection in a world where people were often more interested in status than genuine meaning.

As they talked, Isabella felt a growing connection with Lucas, a feeling of mutual understanding that seemed to transcend the social barriers that normally separated them. There was something deeply comforting about finding someone who seemed to understand your inner struggles and share a similar outlook on what really mattered in life.

Lucas, in turn, began to realize that Isabella was not just a figure of luxury and status, but a real person with feelings and insecurities. The way she talked about her frustrations and desires gave him a new perspective on the world he had begun to question. He felt a growing attraction to Isabella, not just for her beauty and charm, but for the depth of her personality and the authenticity she seemed to represent.

As the night progressed, the conversation between Isabella and Lucas deepened, and the connection between them became more evident. There was a sense that something important was emerging, a mutual understanding and connection that seemed to defy established norms. However, there was also an awareness that this connection was being tested by their respective realities and expectations.

The art exhibition ended, and Isabella and Lucas said

goodbye with the promise to continue the conversation at another time. There was a sense of anticipation in the air, a recognition that what was beginning to develop between them could be something truly special, but also challenging.

As Isabella returned to her mansion, she reflected on the night and her growing connection with Lucas. There was a part of her that wanted to explore this new relationship, but there was also a growing concern about how it might impact her life and the expectations her parents and society had for her. Doubt and uncertainty were mixed with a new sense of hope and possibility.

Lucas, in turn, returned to his apartment with a feeling of satisfaction and anxiety. The conversation with Isabella had been a revelation, and he felt a growing need to understand where this could lead. He knew he was entering uncharted territory, but the prospect of exploring this new connection with Isabella was a source of excitement and anticipation.

"The Look of Nonconformity" represents the beginning of a profound emotional journey for Isabella and Lucas, where their connection becomes a powerful force that challenges their lives and their perspectives. As they continue to explore this new relationship, they will face challenges and questions that will test the strength of their feelings and their ability to overcome the barriers imposed by their different realities. Their journey is just beginning, and the road ahead is full of promise, doubt, and the possibility of finding something truly transformative.

CHAPTER 3: ECHOES OF A DECISION

The city of New York, vibrant and incessant, moved at its normal pace, but for Isabella and Lucas, the consequences of their meeting at the gallery were far from simple or predictable. Both were immersed in a whirlwind of feelings and reflections, each struggling to understand the profound impact this new connection was beginning to have on their lives.

For Isabella Montgomery, the routine of her high society life continued to be marked by social events and prestigious engagements. However, Lucas' presence in her mind became a constant reminder that there was something outside the norm that she needed to explore. Work meetings with her parents and planned social engagements were interrupted by thoughts of the young entrepreneur who had managed to awaken a part of her that she had kept repressed for too long.

Her weekly lunch with her mother, Caroline Montgomery, was approaching, and Isabella knew she couldn't escape the usual questions about her future plans and social expectations. The lunch table was laid out with the usual precision and refinement, and the atmosphere was marked by an atmosphere of formality and expectations.

Caroline, with her attentive gaze and impeccable posture, didn't miss the opportunity to start the conversation with a question that seemed inevitable. "Isabella, dear, how have you been feeling since the gala? Your parents and I look forward to learning more about your future plans. Is there anything new in your life?"

Isabella hesitated for a moment, trying to decide how much she should reveal about what was happening to her. Her mind was occupied with thoughts about Lucas, and she knew her answers might reveal more than planned. However, to her surprise, the desire to be honest and open was stronger than the impulse to keep up appearances.

"Actually, Mom, the event was quite eye-opening," Isabella began, trying to maintain a casual tone. "I met someone interesting. He's an entrepreneur in the technology sector and… well, we had a pretty in-depth conversation about life and our own pursuits."

Caroline raised an eyebrow, her interest immediately piqued. "Oh, really? And what do you think about him? Does he seem like a good catch?"

Her mother's question was clear, but Isabella felt a mixture of discomfort and curiosity. "He's very different from what I'm used to seeing. There is an authenticity to him that is rare among people we know in our social circles. I feel like there's something more at play here, but I'm still trying to figure out what it is."

Caroline watched her daughter with a look that mixed interest and concern. "Isabella, it's great that you're open to new experiences and meeting different people. However, remember that our choices have implications and that we must consider their impact on our lives and the future. You must make decisions that are aligned with your goals and what is expected of you."

The conversation with her mother left Isabella feeling uncomfortable. She wasn't ready to face the social pressures and expectations her family imposed, especially when she was beginning to explore something so new and potentially transformative. The struggle between her personal desires and family expectations was becoming increasingly evident.

Meanwhile, Lucas was facing an equally tumultuous day at work. His office, a sleek, modern building in midtown Manhattan, was buzzing with activities and high-stakes appointments. However, even with the intense workload, his mind couldn't get away from thinking about Isabella. Her authenticity and the connection they had shared had marked him in unexpected ways.

Lucas found a moment of calm in the midst of the office chaos to reflect on what had happened. He knew he needed to act cautiously and strategically, especially since Isabella's life was immersed in a social sphere that was very different from his own. The difference in backgrounds and social pressure represented significant barriers that needed to be considered.

The decision on how to proceed was complex. Lucas knew that for any meaningful relationship to flourish, he needed to better understand what Isabella wanted and what he was willing to go through to build something real. However, there was a part of him that felt the risk would be worth it, and the attraction to Isabella made him want to explore that connection further.

After much reflection, Lucas decided to take action. He sent a message to Isabella, inviting her to an informal dinner at a small, cozy restaurant that he knew offered a quiet, intimate atmosphere. The idea was to create a space where they could talk in more depth, away from the eyes and pressure of grand social events.

Isabella received the invitation with a mixture of anticipation and apprehension. She was eager to see Lucas again and continue exploring the connection they had begun to develop, but she also felt a certain trepidation about how this meeting might develop. She knew she needed to be honest with herself and Lucas about her feelings and expectations.

On the night of the meeting, Isabella prepared herself with special care. She opted for an elegant but simple dress that reflected a more personal and genuine approach than the usual glamor of social events. Lucas, for his part, chose a casual yet sophisticated attire that reflected his desire to create a comfortable and authentic environment for conversation.

The restaurant, tucked away on a quiet city street, offered a welcoming atmosphere and an atmosphere that seemed conducive to meaningful conversation. When Isabella arrived, she was greeted by Lucas with a warm smile and a look that conveyed a sincere desire to connect.

Dinner began in a relaxed manner, with an exchange of comments about the atmosphere and the dishes. As the night progressed, the conversation deepened and personal topics began to surface. Isabella and Lucas shared stories about their childhoods, their challenges and their hopes for the future. Each revelation brought a new layer to their connection, strengthening mutual understanding and respect.

Isabella spoke about the pressure of meeting her family's expectations and the struggle to find a balance between what was expected of her and what she really wanted. Lucas, in turn, spoke about the challenges of navigating a competitive business world and the difficulty of finding people with whom he could have a true connection.

The dinner ended with a sense of satisfaction and a deeper understanding between the two. They left the restaurant with a renewed sense of hope and a promise to continue exploring this new relationship. They were both aware that the journey ahead would be challenging, but they were willing to face the obstacles to discover what could develop between them.

"Echoes of a Decision" marks a pivotal moment in Isabella and Lucas' story, where their choices and decisions begin to shape the future of their connection. The internal struggle and external pressures they face are a reflection of the complexities of love and social expectations, and their decision to continue exploring this new relationship represents a significant step in their personal journeys. The path ahead is full of uncertainties and challenges, but their determination to seek something true and meaningful will be the key to overcoming the barriers and finding what really matters.

CHAPTER 4: SECRETS OF A PAST

With the beginning of a new month, Isabella and Lucas' lives continued to be marked by an intertwining of challenges and discoveries. The impact of the previous encounter had laid a foundation for what promised to be a complex and emotionally charged journey. Both were now trying to understand what this new connection meant and how it fit into their lives filled with responsibilities and expectations.

Isabella Montgomery awoke to a cloudy morning, New York City shrouded in a subtle haze that seemed to reflect her emotional state. Despite the beauty of the city, a feeling of disorientation accompanied it. She was preparing for another day of social engagements and business responsibilities, but her mind was occupied with thoughts about Lucas and the deep conversation they had shared the night before.

After a quick breakfast and a meeting with her company's team, Isabella decided she needed a moment to herself. The constant pressure of meeting family and societal expectations had left her feeling tired and confused. She needed space to reflect on what she really wanted and how Lucas' presence in her life could influence her future decisions.

His choice was to spend the afternoon in a small park close to his home. The park, with its winding trails and serene rest areas, offered a refuge from urban chaos and constant pressure. As she walked, Isabella thought about Lucas and the growing connection between them. She remembered the way he made her feel seen and understood in a way few others could. There was something deeply attractive about her authenticity and her way of living, but there was also a growing concern about how the relationship might affect her already established life.

Meanwhile, Lucas Ferreira was immersed in an equally intense work routine. The office was buzzing with activities and meetings, but his mind couldn't get away from thoughts of Isabella. He knew he needed to find a way to continue exploring this new connection, but he was aware that the path wouldn't be easy.

After a series of meetings and conference calls, Lucas found a quiet moment to reflect. He remembered how the conversation with Isabella had revealed a vulnerability and a desire for connection that he rarely found in his social circle. Her authenticity was a welcome contrast to the superficiality that often dominated her world. But for anything meaningful to develop, he needed to better understand what was really at stake and how his own insecurities and past could influence the future.

Deciding to take an important step, Lucas began exploring the idea of sharing more about his own past with Isabella. He knew that honesty and transparency were essential to building a real connection, and he was determined not to let secrets and insecurities stop him from moving forward. There were aspects of his past that he had kept hidden, and now seemed like the time to reveal them.

While Lucas pondered how to approach the subject, Isabella continued to reflect on her own discoveries. In the park, while sitting on a bench, she revisited memories of her childhood and youth. The way her life had been shaped by family and social expectations made her realize how much she had sacrificed because of these demands. The authenticity Lucas represented felt like an escape, but she also wondered if she was ready for the challenges that might come with following that path.

The afternoon in the park gave way to a peaceful evening, and Isabella decided it was time to face the issues that had been tormenting her. She felt she needed a frank conversation with Lucas, where they could explore her concerns and expectations in more depth.

Lucas, in turn, was also ready to take this step. He had decided it was time to open himself up completely to Isabella and share what was truly stored in his heart. Honesty was the only way to build a solid foundation for what was to come, and he was prepared to face any backlash that might come his way.

That same night, Lucas invited Isabella to a new meeting, this time in a more personal location. He chose a quiet cafe known for its cozy, low-key atmosphere. The place was a refuge from the hustle and bustle of the city, and offered the perfect setting for meaningful conversation.

When Isabella arrived at the cafe, she was greeted by Lucas with a sincere smile and a look that conveyed a desire for vulnerability and honesty. They sat at a private table, away from the hustle and bustle of the café, and began their conversation with a sense of anticipation and apprehension.

Lucas was the first to speak. "Isabella, before we start, I wanted to say that it has been really important for me to share this connection with you. But there are also things about me that I feel you need to know, so we can have a solid foundation for what's to come."

Isabella looked at him with a look of understanding and encouragement. "I also feel like it's important to be completely honest with each other. What would you like to share?"

Lucas took a deep breath and began to share parts of his past that he had kept hidden. He spoke about the difficulties he faced growing up in a less privileged environment, and how these experiences shaped his vision of success and his insecurities. He also revealed some of his past failures and mistakes, and how these moments had helped him grow and understand what really mattered in life.

Isabella listened attentively, feeling a mixture of empathy and admiration for Lucas. His honesty was a reflection of the vulnerability and authenticity that she had found so attractive. She realized that despite the differences in their life stories, there was a genuine connection that transcended circumstances and expectations.

After Lucas finished sharing, Isabella decided it was time to also open up about her own insecurities and challenges. He shared with Lucas the pressures he faced to meet family and social expectations, and how this had impacted his perception of love and happiness. He talked about his doubts and fears about the future and how his presence was beginning to influence his decisions and feelings.

The conversation deepened, and they both began to explore the challenges they could face if they decided to continue investing in the connection they had started to build. They openly discussed their expectations and concerns, and how they could deal with the external and internal pressures that would arise.

Dinner was an opportunity for both of them to get to

know each other more deeply and strengthen the foundation of their relationship. While there was an awareness that the journey ahead would be complex and challenging, there was also a sense of hope and determination to face the obstacles together.

"Secrets of the Past" marks a pivotal moment in Isabella and Lucas' journey, where honesty and vulnerability become essential to developing a true connection. As they share their pasts and face the realities of their lives, they begin to build a solid foundation for the future, even amid the uncertainties and challenges that lie ahead. Their journey is just beginning, and the decisions they make will be instrumental in shaping what develops between them.

CHAPTER 5: THE GAME OF APPEARANCES

As autumn settled in New York, bringing a blanket of gold and red to the city's trees, Isabella and Lucas' lives continued to intertwine in an intricate game of appearances and reality. The glamor of their worlds, personal challenges, and social expectations created a complex tapestry that they were both trying to decipher. With each step, the line between desire and reality became thinner, and the game of appearances seemed a constant threat to the authenticity they were trying to preserve.

Isabella Montgomery was now in the midst of one of the busiest seasons on the high society social calendar. Charity events, galas, and corporate engagements were piling up, and each one seemed to require a new mask for her to wear. As she prepared for a charity reception at one of the city's most renowned clubs, the pressure of maintaining a perfect image consumed her.

She wore a stunning evening gown, with beaded details and an elegant neckline, reflecting the glow of the lights around her. The dress was a work of art that matched the opulence of the event, but behind the facade of perfection, Isabella felt a growing uneasiness. The superficial conversations, the forced smiles and the constant need to live up to expectations seemed far from the sincere connection she had found with Lucas.

Upon arriving at the club, Isabella was greeted by a series of greetings and small talk, each a reminder of the difference between the world she found herself in and the one she had experienced with Lucas. She participated in a series of conversations and interactions, but her mind was always focused on meeting him, which seemed like a refuge from the game of appearances that dominated her social life.

Meanwhile, Lucas Ferreira was embroiled in his own battle against appearances and expectations. After a day full of meetings and business decisions, he found himself reflecting on how to balance his personal life with the demands of his job. Her world was different from Isabella's, but the pressure to maintain an image of success and control was also intense.

He had decided to prepare for the next stage of his journey with Isabella. The authenticity she represented was something he deeply valued, and he wanted to find a way to integrate that authenticity into his business world and social expectations. For him, this meant facing the dissonance between what was real and what was superficial.

The charity event that Isabella was participating in was, for Lucas, an opportunity to take a closer look at the world in which she moved. He knew that understanding the social dynamics and expectations Isabella faced would be crucial in helping them navigate these challenges together. With this in mind, Lucas decided it would be best to attend the event, not just as an observer, but as someone who could connect more deeply with Isabella's reality.

Upon arriving at the club, Lucas was impressed by the

grandeur and glamor of the environment. The exquisite decor, elegant clothing and distinguished guests created an atmosphere of exclusivity and opulence. He knew that for Isabella, this environment was familiar, but for him, it was a new and fascinating world.

Lucas watched as Isabella interacted with other guests. He noticed the way she moved easily between conversations and smiles, maintaining a facade of perfection that, he knew, didn't fully reflect what she felt inside. There was a clear contrast between the Isabella he knew in his private moments and the Isabella who presented herself in public.

Determined to find a moment to connect with her, Lucas looked for an opportunity to get closer. When he finally found a more reserved space in the club, he approached Isabella with a sincere smile. "Isabella, it's a pleasure to see you here. May I accompany you for a moment?"

Isabella looked at him with a relieved smile, grateful to have a moment of genuine connection amid the superficiality of the event. "Of course, Lucas. I was waiting for a moment to escape this routine of appearances."

The two headed to a quieter area of the club, where they could talk without the constant pressure of social expectations. Lucas began sharing his observations about the event and the social dynamics he had noticed. "It's fascinating to see how everyone here behaves. The way people present themselves and interact is almost like a carefully choreographed ballet. It seems that authenticity is a rarity."

Isabella smiled with an expression of understanding. "And truth. I often feel like I'm living in a play, with each of us playing a specific role. Sometimes it's hard to remember who we really are when we're so caught up in the appearance game."

Their conversation flowed with an honesty and depth that seemed almost palpable. They discussed how the world around them often overlapped with their true identity and how finding moments of authenticity amidst this was a constant challenge. There was a sense of relief in sharing these reflections with someone who seemed to understand the complexity of the situation.

As they talked, Lucas shared his own struggles with maintaining authenticity in a business world where image was often as important as the actual content. He talked about how, despite apparent success, he often felt disconnected from his own true aspirations and values.

Isabella listened intently, feeling a growing connection with Lucas. His sincerity was a refreshing contrast to the superficiality she faced daily, and she appreciated the way he approached these issues with an honest and thoughtful perspective.

The event continued, but for Isabella and Lucas, the true moment of connection had occurred away from the prying eyes and superficial conversations. They had found a space where they could be real with each other, and it strengthened the foundation of their relationship.

As the event drew to a close, Isabella and Lucas said goodbye with a promise to continue exploring this new connection. They knew they would face challenges and pressures along the way, but they were determined to keep authenticity and sincerity as pillars of their relationship.

"The Game of Appearances" is a chapter that explores the complexity of social expectations and pressures to maintain a perfect image. As Isabella and Lucas navigated this world of superficiality, they found moments of true connection and understanding. The challenge of balancing appearances with authenticity continues to be a central theme in their journey, and the decisions they make as they move forward will be crucial in shaping the future of their relationship. The path ahead is full of uncertainty, but the search for genuine connection is what guides them through the challenges and pressures they face.

CHAPTER 6: BETWEEN LUXURY AND TRUTH

The month of November brought a cold breeze and gray skies to New York, as if the city was reflecting the internal storm brewing in Isabella and Lucas' lives. The deep connection they had begun to explore was now being challenged by new revelations and the complexities that emerged as their relationship progressed.

Isabella Montgomery was busy with preparations for a large charity gala that her family organized annually. The gala was one of the most important events on the social calendar and was a reflection of the Montgomery family's wealth and status. Despite the importance of the event, Isabella was increasingly aware of how luxury and appearances were beginning to take a toll on her life, especially in contrast to the authenticity she had found with Lucas.

The day of the gala was approaching, and Isabella spent long hours coordinating details, making sure everything was perfect. The pressure to maintain a flawless image was intense, and she began to feel the weight of responsibility on her shoulders. Amidst the chaos of preparations, she found moments of tranquility in thoughts of Lucas, wishing he was by her side to support her.

Lucas Ferreira, in turn, continued to adapt to Isabella's world, observing and trying to understand the complexity of appearances and social expectations that surrounded her life. He was determined to support Isabella, but he was also beginning to question the impact this relationship could have on his own life and values.

While Isabella dealt with the frenzy of preparations for the gala, Lucas made an important decision. He wanted to show Isabella that he was committed to understanding her world, but he also needed to confront his own feelings and expectations. With that in mind, he decided to surprise Isabella, planning a special night that could help them escape the pressure of the outside world and focus on the genuine connection they were trying to build.

The night before the gala, Lucas prepared an intimate dinner in a cozy restaurant, away from the spotlight and social hustle and bustle. He chose a restaurant with a quiet, elegant atmosphere where they could enjoy a delicious meal without the distractions of appearances.

Isabella received Lucas' invitation with a smile of relief. After weeks of intense preparation for the gala, the idea of having a night dedicated to herself and her connection with Lucas was a welcome relief. She dressed in a simple yet sophisticated dress that reflected her desire to distance herself from luxury and appearances for a moment.

Upon arriving at the restaurant, Isabella found Lucas waiting for her with a warm smile. He led her to a candlelit table, where a warm atmosphere and soft music created the perfect setting for a heartfelt conversation.

"Isabella, I'm glad you could come. I wanted us to have a moment for ourselves, away from all the hustle and bustle and expectations. Sometimes, it's easy to get lost in appearances and forget what really matters," Lucas said, as he pulled out the chair for her.

Isabella sat down, feeling a sense of gratitude and comfort at being with Lucas in such a personal setting. "Thank you, Lucas. I really needed this. The gala is important, but sometimes I feel like I'm living in a world of appearances and that I get lost in the middle of it all."

During dinner, the two discussed not only the gala and the social world Isabella was in, but also their feelings about what was happening between them. Lucas talked about his own worries and insecurities, and how he was beginning to feel like his own life was being shaped by external expectations.

Isabella listened intently, appreciating Lucas's honesty and vulnerability. She shared her feelings of being torn between the desire to be authentic and the need to meet the social expectations of her family and society. Their conversation was an opportunity to explore more deeply what it meant to be true to oneself in a world that constantly pushed for perfection.

As the night progressed, Isabella and Lucas began to talk about their dreams and aspirations, away from external pressures. They discussed what they really wanted in their lives and how they could find a balance between luxury and truth. There was a sense of hope and renewal as they shared their deepest desires and discovered that their aspirations aligned in surprising ways.

When dinner came to an end, Lucas made a loving gesture, presenting Isabella with a small package. When she opened it, she found an elegant necklace with a pendant that represented a symbol of commitment and connection. "I wanted you to have something that represented what we have. Something that symbolizes our journey together and the desire to find truth and authenticity amidst luxury and appearances."

Isabella was moved by the gesture and the meaning behind the gift. "It's beautiful, Lucas. And it means a lot to me. Thank you for reminding me of what's really important and for being there for me as we navigate it all."

On the night of the gala, Isabella looked radiant in a stunning evening gown, but Lucas' gift and their special night together gave her a new perspective on the event. She felt a renewed sense of authenticity and connection, which helped her face the demands of the gala with a renewed sense of purpose.

The gala was a success, with an atmosphere of glamor and sophistication that reflected the Montgomery family's status. However, for Isabella, the true value of the evening lay in the deep connection she had shared with Lucas and the sense that, despite appearances, there was something true and meaningful in her life.

"Between Luxury and Truth" is a chapter that explores the tension between external appearances and the search for authenticity. As Isabella and Lucas continue to face the pressures of their social worlds, they find moments of truth and connection that help them navigate these challenges. Their relationship is tested and strengthened by these experiences, and they begin to discover how to balance luxury and truth in their lives. The path ahead promises more challenges and discoveries, but the commitment to finding authenticity amid appearances remains the guide for your journey.

CHAPTER 7: SECRETS REVEALED

Winter was beginning to settle in New York, bringing with it an atmosphere of expectation and mystery. The cold weather and short days seemed to reflect the growing tension in Isabella and Lucas' lives. As their relationship deepened, previously hidden secrets began to emerge, challenging their perceptions and testing their connection.

The month of December brought with it the season of parties and social events, and Isabella was immersed in preparations for the Montgomery family's annual winter ball. This event had been a tradition for generations and a showcase for the family's status and wealth. Isabella felt the pressure of keeping her image impeccable, but the recent discovery of an unexpected secret was weighing heavily on her shoulders.

During an intimate conversation with Lucas the night before, Isabella had revealed to him a part of her past that she had never shared with anyone. She spoke about a troubled relationship from her youth, a relationship that had left deep emotional scars and a distrust of others. This secret, which she had kept hidden for years, now seemed to be influencing her outlook on life and her current relationships.

Lucas, upon hearing Isabella's confession, felt a wave of empathy and concern. The revelation made her realize the complexity of Isabella's life and the weight of the secrets she carried. He was determined to support her and help her face these challenges, but he knew that the truth was a crucial factor in building a solid future together.

As Isabella prepared for the ball, she was absorbed in a mixture of anxiety and anticipation. Preparations for the event were meticulous and required meticulous attention to detail. The hall was being decorated with a splendor that reflected the luxury and opulence of the Montgomery family, and Isabella went out of her way to make sure everything was perfect.

However, preparing for the ball wasn't just about appearance; it was also an opportunity to face some of the secrets that had emerged. Isabella knew she needed to find a way to reconcile her past with her present and to face the truths that were beginning to reveal themselves.

On the eve of the ball, Lucas decided to surprise Isabella with a gesture that could alleviate some of the weight she was carrying. He arranged a special evening in a quiet restaurant, similar to the one they had met in previously. He wanted to create a space where Isabella could feel comfortable sharing more about her feelings and challenges.

When Isabella arrived at the restaurant, she was greeted by Lucas with a warm smile and a comforting hug. The soft, welcoming atmosphere seemed a welcome contrast to the hustle and bustle and stress surrounding the ball.

"Thank you for giving me this night, Lucas. I need

this more than you know," said Isabella, as she made herself comfortable at the table.

Lucas smiled and held Isabella's hand. "I wanted you to know that I'm here for you, no matter what's going on. If there's anything else you need to share or face, I'm there for you."

During dinner, Isabella continued to open her heart to Lucas. She talked about the challenges she had faced in her past relationship, how those challenges had shaped her, and how they were still influencing her current choices and emotions. She discussed the fear of repeating past mistakes and the difficulty of fully trusting someone, even in a relationship that felt true and sincere.

Lucas listened attentively, offering words of support and understanding. He spoke about the importance of facing and overcoming the past to enable a healthier and more fulfilling future. He also shared his own experiences and challenges, revealing how he had learned to deal with his own insecurities and fears.

The conversation was deep and revealing, and helped Isabella feel lighter and more connected to Lucas. She began to realize that despite the secrets and challenges, there was a solid foundation of understanding and support between them.

However, as the night progressed, Isabella received a call that left her deeply disturbed. It was from his mother, who informed him that there was an unexpected problem with preparations for the ball. Something had gone wrong with the decorations and some of the vendors, and there was a threat that the event might not go ahead as planned.

Isabella felt a wave of panic, knowing the situation was out of her control. She tried to handle the situation calmly, but the pressure and responsibility were becoming overwhelming. Lucas noticed Isabella's anguish and offered his unconditional support.

"We'll solve this together," Lucas said with determination. "No matter what happens, I will be by your side."

The night turned into a race against time, with Lucas and Isabella working together to resolve the issues and ensure the prom could go ahead. They faced a range of challenges, from coordinating supplier replacements to dealing with unexpected logistical issues. The experience was exhausting, but it was also a test of the commitment and collaboration they had developed.

At the end of the night, despite the obstacles faced, the dance was a success. The decor was fixed and the event was held with the opulence and glamor that was expected. Isabella felt relieved and grateful to have Lucas by her side during this crisis. The experience also served as a reminder that facing challenges together can strengthen a relationship and create even deeper bonds.

After the event, as the guests began to disperse, Isabella and Lucas found a moment of tranquility in the most private corner of the room. They reflected on the night and the experiences they had shared. Isabella expressed her gratitude to Lucas for his support and for being there during such a difficult time.

"I don't know what I would have done without you, Lucas. Your support means more to me than I can express," Isabella said, looking Lucas in the eye.

Lucas smiled and held Isabella's hand. "I'm here for you, always. Truth and transparency are the foundation of our relationship, and I am committed to facing any challenge alongside you."

"Secrets Revealed" is a chapter that explores the complexity of the secrets and hidden truths that impact the lives of Isabella and Lucas. As they face challenges and revelations, their relationship is tested and strengthened. The chapter illustrates how facing the past and challenges together can deepen the connection between two people and help build a solid foundation for the future. Isabella and Lucas' journey is far from simple, but their commitment to facing truths and challenges together guides them through difficulties and uncertainties.

CHAPTER 8: THE PRICE OF TRUTH

The start of the new year brought with it a wave of renewal and promise, but for Isabella and Lucas, it also brought an unexpected challenge that threatened to shake the foundations of their relationship. The holiday season was now behind them, and they were both trying to regain some normalcy in their lives, but the echoes of the recent revelations and tensions still reverberated in their hearts and minds.

The month of January brought a new chill, and New York City seemed quieter after the frenzy of festivities. Isabella and Lucas found a brief moment of calm amidst the chaos of the beginning of the year, taking advantage of a peaceful morning to explore the city. It was a welcome break from social obligations and an opportunity to reconnect in a more personal setting.

As they strolled through Central Park, the cloudy sky and cold breeze created a moody but also reflective atmosphere. Lucas and Isabella talked about their plans for the year and how they could continue to strengthen their relationship. They were determined to face the challenges together, but they knew there were still issues to be resolved.

In the middle of the conversation, Isabella received a message that left her visibly disturbed. It was from an unexpected source – an old friend of her family who had delicate information about Isabella's past. The message mentioned an imminent meeting and suggested there were details Isabella needed to know.

Isabella tried to hide her concern, but Lucas noticed her discomfort and asked what was happening. With a sigh, Isabella explained the message and revealed that there was a part of her past that she had not yet shared with him – a part that involved an old debt owed to her family and a secret that had been carefully hidden.

"I don't know what could be going on, but this situation seems more complicated than I imagined," said Isabella, looking at Lucas with a mixture of anxiety and sadness.

Lucas held Isabella's hand with a comforting gesture. "Whatever it is, we will face it together. The truth can be hard to deal with, but we are stronger when we are there for each other."

Determined to discover the truth, Isabella and Lucas decided to go to the meeting scheduled with their old family friend. They met at a chic Upper East Side cafe, a place that seemed like a safe haven for delicate conversations. The atmosphere was sophisticated, but also inviting, providing a suitable setting for revealing secrets.

When they arrived at the cafe, they were greeted by Helena, their old family friend. She was an elegant woman with an imposing presence, with an aura of mystery that made Isabella feel even more apprehensive. Helena led them to a private table, where they could talk in privacy.

After the initial greetings, Helena began to talk about

Isabella's past and her family. She revealed details that Isabella had tried to forget – a significant debt incurred by the Montgomery family years ago, which had led to a series of complications and tensions. The debt, which had been paid off, had repercussions that Isabella was unaware of, but which were now coming to light.

"I understand that this may be difficult to hear," said Helena, looking at Isabella with an expression of understanding. "But there are details that need to be clarified. The truth about the past can impact the present and future in ways you need to consider."

Isabella was shocked by the revelation and felt a mixture of shame and anger. The feeling of having been deceived or kept in the dark about something so significant was painful. Lucas noticed Isabella's difficulty and went out of his way to offer support, but he was also beginning to wonder about the impact of these revelations on his own life and his relationship with Isabella.

As Helena continued to explain the situation, Isabella began to reflect on how past actions had shaped her life and current relationships. She thought about the pressure her family had placed on her to keep up appearances and how that had affected her own choices and values.

After listening to the information and asking some questions, Isabella and Lucas thanked Helena for her honesty and revealing the secrets. They knew they needed to process what they had learned and decide how to move forward. The conversation left Isabella with a feeling of disorientation, but also with a desire to face the truth head on and deal with the consequences.

After the meeting, Isabella and Lucas left the cafe and walked through the streets of New York, absorbing the impact of the revelations. Isabella was silent, deep in thought, while Lucas tried to find the right words to offer support.

"I feel like everything is falling apart," said Isabella finally, her voice breaking. "I didn't know that my family's past had so many secrets. Now I feel like I can't trust anything I thought I knew."

Lucas stopped and turned to Isabella, holding her face in his hands with an expression of affection. "The truth can be painful, but it is also an important step towards healing and building a stronger future. No matter what the past has brought, we are here for each other. Together, we can face anything."

The conversation between Isabella and Lucas was an opportunity to explore how to deal with the truth and how to find a way forward. They discussed the importance of facing the past with courage and building a foundation of trust and transparency in their relationship.

Chapter 8, **"The Price of Truth,"** explores the complexity of the revelations and hidden truths that emerge in the lives of Isabella and Lucas. The discovery of secrets from the past leads to a reevaluation of your own beliefs and values, and the challenge of coming to terms with these truths tests the strength and depth of your relationship. The chapter illustrates how truth, although often painful and disconcerting, can be a powerful tool for healing and building a more authentic and meaningful future. Isabella and Lucas' journey continues to be marked by challenges and discoveries, and their commitment to facing the truth together guides them through the difficulties they encounter.

CHAPTER 9:
BROKEN TIES

Winter seemed to have deepened, reflecting the atmosphere of uncertainty that hung over Isabella and Lucas. The weight of the secrets revealed had left an indelible mark on their lives, and the sense of discomfort was palpable. They tried to find stability amid the turmoil, but the reality was that the truth was not just a revelation – it was also an ongoing challenge.

In the days that followed after the meeting with Helena, Isabella and Lucas felt the need to distance themselves from the city and its problems. They decided to spend a weekend at a small country house outside of New York, hoping to find a temporary refuge where they could reflect and reconnect without the distractions and pressures of everyday life.

The cottage was situated in a picturesque area, surrounded by snow-covered trees and with a stunning view of the hills in the distance. The peace and quiet of the environment offered a welcome contrast to the frenzy of the city. Isabella and Lucas arrived at the place on Friday afternoon, and a feeling of tranquility began to envelop their hearts.

As they explored the house, Isabella came across a small library filled with old and classic books. She lost herself in her reading for a moment, looking for an escape in literature to help process her emotions. Lucas, in turn, dedicated himself to preparing a special meal for the evening, trying to create a welcoming and romantic atmosphere.

Over dinner, while enjoying a simple, home-cooked meal, Isabella and Lucas talked about recent events and how they could find a way forward. Isabella was still processing the impact of the revelations about her family's past and felt the need to better understand how it related to her current life.

"I feel like the past is haunting us in many ways," said Isabella, looking at her plate with a thoughtful look. "My family's debt and the secrets that were revealed seem to have such a huge influence on the present. It's hard to know who to trust and what to believe."

Lucas, who had maintained a supportive and understanding attitude, responded with a deep reflection. "The past can have a powerful influence, but it also has the ability to teach us and strengthen us. Facing these truths is challenging, but it can help us find a clearer path forward. We need to be willing to learn from the past and let go of the things that no longer serve our growth."

As the night progressed, Isabella and Lucas found themselves chatting by the fireplace, where the heat and light created an intimate and comforting atmosphere. The conversation delved into personal issues and how current challenges were shaping their perceptions and emotions.

During this conversation, Isabella mentioned a specific aspect of her past that was beginning to emerge more clearly:

the expectations placed on her by her family and how these had influenced her life choices and relationships. She revealed that, from a young age, she had felt pressured to maintain a perfect image and deal with issues of status and reputation, often at the expense of her own happiness and authenticity.

Lucas listened intently, offering words of encouragement and understanding. He was beginning to realize the depth of the issues Isabella faced and the complexity of the expectations that had shaped her life.

"I understand how overwhelming these pressures can be," Lucas said, looking into Isabella's eyes. "But you are more than any expectation or image. The true essence of who you are is within you, and that's what matters. We must focus on being authentic and building a life that makes us happy, regardless of external expectations."

The intimate conversation and deep connection they shared helped alleviate some of the emotional weight Isabella was carrying. However, the feeling of discomfort did not completely disappear, and Isabella and Lucas were still struggling to find a way to deal with the complexities of their pasts and their feelings.

The next morning, Isabella and Lucas decided to explore the area around the cottage. They walked through the snow, breathing in the fresh air and enjoying the natural beauty around them. The walk was a time of reflection and connection, and offered a refreshing break from the worries they were facing.

As they walked, Isabella began to talk about her hopes for the future and how she wanted to find a way to reconcile her past with her aspirations and dreams. She mentioned wanting to build a life that was truly authentic and meaningful, rather than conforming to expectations imposed by her family or society.

"I want to build a future where I can be true to myself

and the people around me," said Isabella with determination. "I want to find a way to leave past expectations behind and create something that truly makes me happy."

Lucas smiled and held Isabella's hand. "I want that for us too. Let's work together to build a life that reflects our true passions and values. No matter what the future brings, we will face it together and with courage."

Chapter 9, **"Broken Ties,"** explores Isabella and Lucas' journey as they face the challenges and complexities of their pasts. The search for temporary refuge offers an opportunity to reflect and reconnect, but it also reveals the depth of the issues they face. Intimate conversation and personal exploration help illuminate the importance of being authentic and building a future based on personal values and passions. The chapter illustrates the struggle to find stability and meaning amidst difficulties and how the deep connection between Isabella and Lucas helps them face challenges and seek a more authentic and fulfilling future.

CHAPTER 10: SHADOWS OF THE PAST

The beginning of February brought with it an air of renewal and hope. Winter was in full swing, and New York City was covered in a blanket of snow that made it an enchanting scene. However, for Isabella and Lucas, the beautiful setting could not hide the shadows of the past that continued to loom over them.

After the weekend at the cottage, Isabella and Lucas returned to New York with a new sense of determination. They were more united in their desire to face the past and build a future together, but they knew the road ahead was still full of challenges. The meeting with Helena and the revelations about Isabella's past left a trail of uncertainty, and they were determined to explore these questions more deeply.

The first big test of the new month was a gala event that Isabella and Lucas had planned to attend. The event, which would take place at one of New York's most prestigious clubs, was an opportunity for Isabella to return to her social circle and deal with the expectations and pressures associated with it. For Lucas, it was a chance to observe how Isabella interacted with her world and to better understand the dynamics that involved her.

On the night of the event, the club was stunning, decorated with twinkling lights and an elegance that reflected the opulent world in which Isabella had been raised. The atmosphere was one of sophistication and glamour, but there was also an air of superficiality that seemed to contrast with the depth of the issues Isabella and Lucas were facing.

When they arrived at the club, they were greeted by a warm welcome, but also by the silent pressure of expectations and curious looks. Isabella was dressed in an elegant black velvet dress that accentuated her beauty and social standing, while Lucas opted for a classic suit that matched the refined surroundings.

As they walked around the event, Isabella was approached by several acquaintances and longtime friends. The conversation was polite but often superficial, and Lucas noticed Isabella's difficulty in genuinely connecting with the people around her. The pressure to maintain a perfect image seemed to be a constant in her social life, and Lucas felt a growing sense of discomfort as he saw the impact of this on her.

During a break on the dance floor, Isabella and Lucas moved away from the hustle and bustle to talk in a more private corner. Isabella was visibly tired, and the sparkle in her eyes that had previously been so evident now seemed a little dull.

"I feel like I'm constantly trying hard to fit into a mold that isn't truly mine," Isabella admitted, looking at Lucas with a frustrated expression. "The pressure to maintain a perfect image and meet the expectations of others is exhausting. Sometimes I feel like I'm living a lie."

Lucas held Isabella's hand and looked at her with understanding. "I know it's difficult to deal with these expectations and pressures. But remember that you are more than the image others expect you to be. True happiness comes from being true to yourself and finding a way to live according to your own values and desires."

The intimate and comforting chat was interrupted by a group of guests who approached, and Isabella had to resume her social role. Although he tried to maintain his composure and friendliness, Lucas realized that emotional exhaustion was beginning to affect his behavior.

Later in the evening, Isabella and Lucas were approached by an old family acquaintance, Charles Wentworth, an influential businessman with whom Isabella had maintained a cordial but not particularly close relationship. Charles had a confident smile and an imposing presence, and seemed interested in talking to Isabella about personal and professional matters.

Charles greeted Isabella with a firm handshake and an appraising look. "Isabella, it's a pleasure to see you here. I was looking forward to talking to you about some exciting opportunities that have arisen recently."

The conversation quickly turned to more personal terrain. Charles mentioned some rumors that had circulated about Isabella and her family's past, insinuating that he had valuable information and could help resolve some outstanding issues. The mention of rumors and information about the past made Isabella uncomfortable and alert.

"I'm not sure I understand correctly," Isabella replied, trying to remain calm. "What kind of information are you mentioning?"

Charles smiled enigmatically and replied: "Let's say

some information about your family may be closer than you think. Sometimes shadows from the past have a way of surfacing again. And if you're interested, I can offer you a perspective that might help clear some things up."

Isabella felt a chill run down her spine at the suggestion that Charles might be offering something more than just casual conversation. She knew she needed to explore what Charles was implying, but she was also aware that there could be ulterior motives behind his words.

After their conversation with Charles, Isabella and Lucas retreated to a more private area where they were able to discuss what they had just heard. Isabella was worried about the implications of Charles' words and the possibility that he was trying to manipulate the situation for his own interests.

"Charles seems to know more than he's letting on," Isabella said with a worried expression. "I'm not sure I can trust your intentions. The last thing we need is more complications in the middle of all this."

Lucas agreed and expressed the need to be cautious. "We must approach this situation carefully. If Charles really has important information, we need to find out exactly what he knows and what his true interests are. At the same time, we need to be careful not to let this distract us from what really matters – our relationship and our search for a more authentic future."

At the end of the night, Isabella and Lucas returned home with a feeling of uncertainty. The shadows of the past continued to haunt their lives, and Charles' presence brought a new layer of complexity to the situation. They were determined to face the challenges and seek answers, but they also needed to maintain their focus on building a solid and true future.

Chapter 10, **"Shadows of the Past,"** explores Isabella

and Lucas' ongoing struggle to deal with the pressures and expectations that come with social life and the challenges associated with it. The presence of Charles Wentworth and his innuendos add a new dimension of complexity to the plot, requiring Isabella and Lucas to confront issues from the past while trying to preserve their authenticity and integrity. The chapter illustrates how the shadows of the past can have a profound impact on the present and how the search for answers and truth can be a tortuous and challenging path. The connection between Isabella and Lucas is tested, but also reinforced by the need to face these issues together and with courage.

CHAPTER 11:
ENCOUNTERS AND
MISMATCHES

The days following the gala event were a whirlwind of emotions for Isabella and Lucas. Charles Wentworth's suggestion that he had important information about Isabella's past hung over them, creating a cloud of uncertainty that seemed impenetrable. They knew they needed to act cautiously, but they also wanted to better understand the nature of the threats and the secrets that might be hidden.

They decided to start investigating Charles on their own, gathering as much information as possible about the businessman. The first step was to search public records and news sources to obtain a more detailed profile of Charles Wentworth and his connections. Lucas used his research skills and network to compile relevant data, while Isabella sought to understand the context and history of her interaction with Charles.

As they analyzed the information, Isabella and Lucas

began to realize that Charles had a complex reputation. Although he was known for his influence and success in the business world, there were also rumors about his ambition and questionable methods. The exact nature of what he might know about Isabella's past remained hazy, but the growing suspicion that he might be trying to manipulate the situation generated a sense of urgency.

To obtain further clarification, Isabella decided to seek advice from a longtime mentor and family friend, attorney Robert Sinclair. Robert had been a trusted and supportive figure at several critical moments in Isabella's life and was well informed about legal and financial matters.

The meeting with Robert took place in his office, an elegant and sober space in downtown Manhattan. Isabella and Lucas were warmly welcomed by Robert, who showed genuine concern upon hearing about the situation with Charles Wentworth.

"Charles Wentworth is known for being an enigmatic and sometimes manipulative figure," Robert commented, after hearing Isabella's account. "It's possible he's trying to pressure you or exploit some vulnerability. I'll do some checks to better understand the situation and make sure you're protected."

While Robert committed to investigating further, Isabella and Lucas decided to pursue a more proactive approach. They wanted to understand Charles' true intentions and were determined to face any challenge that came their way. The situation was becoming something of a conundrum, and they needed clarity to be able to make informed decisions.

The tension between Isabella and Lucas was also beginning to manifest itself in their relationship. The pressure of dealing with external problems, along with revelations about the past, was creating a dynamic of stress and uncertainty. They encountered moments where mutual support was essential, but they also faced situations where communication became difficult and emotions ran high.

To relieve some of this pressure, Isabella and Lucas decided to take some time for themselves and organize a little getaway. They opted for a relaxing spa retreat in the mountains, where they could find a space to unwind and reconnect in a more peaceful, rejuvenating environment.

The spa was situated in a secluded location surrounded by stunning natural scenery. Isabella and Lucas arrived at the location on Friday afternoon, and the change of environment brought immediate relief. The spa offered a variety of wellness treatments, including massages, thermal baths, and meditation sessions, all designed to help visitors relax and find balance.

During the retreat, Isabella and Lucas took advantage of opportunities to relax and talk about their feelings and concerns. The tranquility of the environment and the treatments on offer provided a welcome break from the pressures and challenges of the outside world.

In one of these conversations, Isabella opened her heart to Lucas about her insecurities and fears about the future. She expressed fear that external pressures and secrets from the past could end up destroying the relationship they were building.

"I really worry about the impact this could all have on us," Isabella said, her voice full of vulnerability. "I feel like we are fighting forces that are beyond our control, and sometimes I worry that this could tear us apart."

Lucas held Isabella's hand and looked at her sincerely. "I understand your fears, but I want you to know that I am here to face this with you. No matter what happens, our love and connection are what matter most. Together, we can overcome any challenge and find a way to build a future that is truly ours."

Lucas' comforting conversation and supportive presence helped Isabella feel calmer and more hopeful. The spa experience brought a new sense of renewal and optimism, and Isabella and Lucas felt they were better prepared to face the challenges that lay ahead.

However, returning to New York brought back the reality of their problems. Robert Sinclair had carried out a preliminary investigation into Charles Wentworth and discovered some revealing information. He arranged a meeting with Isabella and Lucas to discuss his findings.

At the meeting, Robert revealed that Charles was involved in a series of complex investments and financial transactions, some of which appeared questionable and potentially damaging. There were indications that Charles had hidden interests and that he might be seeking to manipulate situations for his own benefits.

"It appears that Charles Wentworth has a history of manipulation and exploitation," Robert explained. "While we don't have all the answers yet, it's important for you to be aware that he may be trying to use your information to get what he wants. I suggest we remain vigilant and careful about what we share with him."

Isabella and Lucas left the meeting with a feeling of relief mixed with concern. The revelation that Charles had questionable intentions confirmed some of their suspicions, but also made it clear that there was still much to discover.

Chapter 11, **"Encounters and Mismatches,"** explores the growing tension in the lives of Isabella and Lucas as they face the challenges posed by social pressures and secrets from their past. The search for clarity and protection, along with trying to find balance amid stress, shows the complexity of your situation. The spa experience offers a moment of renewal and reconnection, but the return to reality highlights the need to face issues with courage and determination. The chapter emphasizes the importance of mutual support and careful vigilance as Isabella and Lucas continue to navigate the complexities of their world and the threats they face.

CHAPTER 12: THE PRICE OF TRUTH

The month of February progressed with an intensity that seemed to reflect the profound changes in Isabella and Lucas' lives. The revelations about Charles Wentworth and the discoveries about his questionable intentions were weighing on them, and the need to clarify the secrets of their past and protect their future was more evident than ever.

With Robert Sinclair's help, Isabella and Lucas had decided to take a more direct approach to confronting Charles. They arranged a meeting with him, determined to find out exactly what his intentions were and what information he possessed. The aim was to ensure that there were no further surprises and that any manipulation or threat was addressed clearly and resolutely.

The meeting was scheduled for a Thursday afternoon, in one of Charles' luxurious offices in the heart of Manhattan. The building was imposing and reflected the businessman's success and wealth. When Isabella and Lucas arrived, they were greeted with formal treatment, which included a receptionist who led them to the conference room where Charles was waiting.

Charles sat at a dark wooden table, surrounded by documents and an aura of authority. His appearance was impeccable, with a well-tailored suit and a calculating smile. He gestured for Isabella and Lucas to sit down and offered them drinks, but the tension in the air was palpable.

"Isabella, Lucas," Charles greeted, his voice carrying a friendly tone, but one that hid a background of calculation. "It's good to see you guys. I hope you have considered what we discussed last time."

Isabella maintained her composure and began the conversation with a direct approach. "Charles, we would like to better understand what you know about our situation and what interest you have in this. Robert Sinclair, our lawyer, did some investigation and discovered that you may have relevant information about my family's past. Can we discuss this openly?"

Charles crossed his arms and smiled, as if he were preparing for a game of chess. "I understand your concern, Isabella. The truth is that there is much more at stake than you might imagine. Your family's past, especially your connection to certain investments and transactions, has implications that may affect not only you, but also other important interests."

Lucas noticed the evasive way in which Charles was referring to the subject and felt the need to press for a more direct answer. "We are here to seek clarity, Charles. If you have information that could affect our lives or our future, we need you to be honest and transparent. We are not willing to play this game without knowing the rules."

Charles adjusted his posture, seeming to consider his words carefully. "The issue is not as simple as it seems. There are complex legal and financial aspects involving your family's past. What I can say is that if you are not careful, you may face consequences that could harm not only you, but also those close to you."

The conversation continued with a tone of increasing tension. Charles was clear in his intentions to maintain control and to use information as a tool of power. However, his lack of clarity and the vague nature of his threats made Isabella and Lucas feel more determined to discover the truth on their own.

After the meeting, Isabella and Lucas returned home with a feeling of frustration and determination. They knew that the situation was far from resolved and that they needed a more effective strategy to deal with Charles' threats and manipulations. Robert Sinclair had suggested that they continue investigating and seek more information about the investments and transactions mentioned by Charles.

Meanwhile, Isabella decided it was time to confront her own family and seek answers directly from her parents. She had avoided many of these topics so as not to cause further concern, but now she felt it was necessary to fully understand the situation and the impact it could have on her life and her relationship with Lucas.

The conversation with his parents took place at a formal dinner at his family home, a historic mansion located in one of New York's most exclusive neighborhoods. Isabella was nervous, but also determined to get answers. Lucas accompanied her, offering support and showing the importance of facing these issues together.

During dinner, Isabella approached the subject with a careful approach, trying not to cause unnecessary discomfort. She began talking about her recent interactions with Charles and expressed her concern about the impact of the information he had revealed.

"I really need to understand more about what Charles Wentworth is implying," Isabella began, looking at her parents seriously. "Is there something in our family's past that could be causing these threats? We need to know the truth to be able to deal with any problem appropriately."

His parents exchanged glances, and the atmosphere in the room became tense. Isabella's mother, Helena, looked hesitant, while her father, Eduardo, wore a worried expression. Finally, it was Eduardo who spoke.

"Isabella, there are things you still don't know about our family's past. Many of them are complicated and involve difficult decisions we have made in the past. We didn't want you to worry about this, but the truth is that some of these issues are coming back to the surface, and we need to deal with them."

The conversation revealed details about past investments and transactions that had involved Isabella's family in complicated situations. There were legal and financial issues that had been resolved discreetly but were now being re-examined due to pressure from Charles.

Isabella and Lucas were shocked by the magnitude of the information revealed, but they also understood the need to confront these issues directly. The impact of the revelations was profound, and they needed to find a way to deal with the consequences and ensure that they were not manipulated or harmed.

Over the next few days, Isabella and Lucas worked with Robert Sinclair to explore the legal and financial implications of the revelations. They spent hours reviewing documents and discussing strategies to protect their interests and ensure that any threat from Charles was met effectively.

Chapter 12, **"The Price of Truth,"** explores the

growing complexity of the situation facing Isabella and Lucas as they deal with threats and revelations about their past. The meeting with Charles Wentworth and the conversation with his parents highlight the importance of facing the truth, even when it is uncomfortable and challenging. Isabella and Lucas' determination to seek clarity and protect their future shows the strength of their relationship and the importance of facing adversity together. The chapter illustrates the ongoing struggle to balance the past and present, and the need for courage and resilience in dealing with challenges posed by external and internal forces.

CHAPTER 13: SHADOWS OF THE PAST

Spring arrived in New York with a promise of renewal and new beginnings. But for Isabella and Lucas, the shadows of the past still hung over them, and the external pressures were far from disappearing. With the details of Charles Wentworth's past transactions and threats finally revealed, the couple were in a race against time to protect their interests and clarify what was really at stake.

Isabella and Lucas had spent the last week delving into legal documents and strategies with Robert Sinclair, trying to understand the complexity of the investments and transactions that had been at the heart of Charles' threats. It was meticulous work that required patience and attention to detail. Each discovery seemed to open new doors to more questions and uncertainties.

In addition to the legal and financial battle, Isabella

was beginning to feel the weight of emotions arising from the revelation of her family's past. She was struggling to maintain her composure and deal with her anxiety, but she was also struggling to keep her relationship with Lucas strong and positive. The stress was affecting their ability to relax and enjoy their moments together, and they were both realizing they needed to find a balance.

One Saturday afternoon, Isabella and Lucas decided to go for a walk in Central Park, trying to escape the pressures and find a moment of tranquility. The sun was shining and the flowers were beginning to bloom, offering a welcome break from the tension they were experiencing.

During the walk, Lucas broke the silence that had settled between them. "You know, Isabella, I really admire the way you're handling all of this. I know it's not easy and the situation is complicated. But her strength and resilience are inspiring."

Isabella smiled, although the worry was still visible in her eyes. "Thank you, Lucas. I just feel like we're on a rollercoaster, and sometimes I wonder if this is all going to end well. But I know we need to face this together, and I'm grateful to have you by my side."

Lucas's support and words provided temporary relief, and the walk in the park helped to clear Isabella's mind a little. However, the return to reality brought back the worries and responsibilities that were waiting.

The following Monday, Robert Sinclair scheduled a meeting to discuss the next steps in the legal strategy. The meeting was held in their office, and Isabella and Lucas were prepared to hear what had been discovered and what the next steps were.

"We have some new information about the

investments and transactions involving your family," Robert began, his tone serious. "While we have no concrete evidence that Charles Wentworth is directly involved in illicit activities, what we have found suggests that he is trying to exploit the situation for his own ends."

Isabella and Lucas listened intently as Robert detailed the findings. There was information about transactions that had been manipulated and investments that were associated with controversial figures. Although there was no direct evidence of corruption or illegality, the complexity of the information raised questions about Charles' potential to manipulate the situation to his advantage.

"We need to be prepared for any eventuality," Robert continued. "This includes the possibility that Charles may attempt to use information to create a scandal or damage his reputation. The best approach is to continue to investigate, ensure all our information is correct, and be ready to act if necessary."

With the action plan outlined, Isabella and Lucas began to focus on a proactive approach. They worked with Robert to ensure that all information was verified and that they were ready for any challenges that might arise. The work was intense and required constant attention, but the determination to protect his future was a powerful motivation.

In addition to the legal and financial issues, Isabella was also beginning to face emotional and psychological pressure. The impact of revelations about her family's past was beginning to weigh on her in unexpected ways. She sought help from a therapist to deal with the emotions and stress she was experiencing.

During therapy sessions, Isabella spoke about the difficulty of dealing with the revelations and the fear that it could affect her relationship with Lucas. The therapist helped Isabella explore her emotions and find ways to manage stress and anxiety.

"It's important to remember that you are not alone on this journey," the therapist advised. "You have Lucas' support and you are doing everything you can to face the situation. Facing these emotions and seeking help is an important part of the healing process and finding a way to move forward."

Isabella found solace in therapy sessions and began to feel a little more emotionally balanced. Professional help offered a new perspective and tools to deal with internal and external pressures.

With progress in the investigations and emotional support, Isabella and Lucas felt more prepared to face the challenges that arose. They continued to work with Robert to ensure all strategies were in place and ready for any eventuality.

However, the threat of Charles Wentworth still loomed over them, and the feeling that they needed to act quickly to protect their future continued. Isabella and Lucas were determined to face the situation head on and ensure they were not manipulated or harmed.

Chapter 13, **"Shadows of the Past,"** explores Isabella and Lucas' struggle to deal with the pressures and challenges posed by revelations about their past and threats from Charles Wentworth. The search for clarity and the need to protect your future show the complexity of the situation and the importance of facing adversity with courage and determination. Emotional experience and professional support offer temporary relief, but the need to continue investigation and prepare for potential challenges highlights the ongoing struggle to find balance and protect what is most important.

CHAPTER 14: ECHOES OF FATE

The month of March brought with it a new wave of challenges and revelations for Isabella and Lucas. With the investigations progressing and pressure from Charles Wentworth still present, the couple felt the urgency to resolve the situation definitively. The past few weeks had been a whirlwind of activity, and the need to find answers and protect their future was more evident than ever.

The atmosphere in Isabella's mansion was charged with tension as she and Lucas reviewed documents and strategies. The home's opulent surroundings, which normally represented comfort and security, now seemed a stage for a constant battle against forces that seemed beyond their control. Every detail of the house, from the towering chandeliers to the luxurious rugs, seemed to reflect the pressure they were both facing.

Lucas had decided it was time to take a more aggressive approach to dealing with Charles' threat. He was determined to gather all the evidence possible to ensure they were not victims of manipulation. With the assistance of Robert Sinclair, they devised a plan to monitor Charles' activities and try to discover if there was any direct connection between him and the suspicious transactions mentioned above.

The first step of the plan involved collecting detailed information about Charles and his financial operations. Lucas hired an experienced private investigator to help follow leads and uncover any relevant information that could be used to strengthen his position. The investigator, a middle-aged man with an impeccable reputation, got to work immediately, scouring financial records and networks of contacts to find anything that could shed light on Charles' true motives.

Meanwhile, Isabella was busy with another important matter: preparing a public defense for any eventuality. She knew that if the situation deteriorated, it would be crucial to be ready to protect her and Lucas's reputation. Working with a public relations specialist, Isabella prepared a series of statements and a communication strategy to face possible attacks or attempts to discredit her name.

Friday afternoon brought a new revelation. The private investigator contacted Lucas to inform him that he had found a significant lead. During an in-depth investigation, he discovered that Charles had recently made a large financial transaction that was linked to an offshore company with a questionable track record. This information could indicate a possible connection between Charles and dubious financial activities.

Lucas and Isabella met with Robert Sinclair to discuss the new discovery. "This financial transaction could be a turning point," Robert explained. "If we can prove that Charles is involved in illicit activities, it could weaken your position and protect you from any manipulation or threats."

Isabella was relieved to have a new lead, but also

worried about the possible repercussions. "What if Charles finds out we're investigating? He may try to act before we have a chance to use this information against him."

Robert agreed. "It's a valid concern. We need to be cautious and ensure our actions are well planned. I will work with the investigator to further analyze and ensure we have sufficient evidence before taking action."

As the investigation continued, Isabella and Lucas faced a new tension: an unexpected visit from an old family friend. Hugo Almeida, an influential businessman and former business partner of Isabella's parents, appeared at the mansion, bringing with him an aura of mystery and concern.

Hugo was a sophisticated-looking man, with a bearing that reflected his experience and success in the business world. He had a reputation for being a discreet and trustworthy person, but the reason for his visit was an enigma. Upon finding him, Isabella and Lucas were immediately alerted by the seriousness of his face.

"Isabella, Lucas," Hugo greeted in a serious tone. "I need to talk to you about something very important. I have received information about Charles Wentworth and his attempt to manipulate the situation involving you. This is not just a business issue; It's personal."

Isabella and Lucas listened intently as Hugo explained that he had received confidential information about Charles from a reliable source. According to Hugo, Charles was planning an action that could have serious consequences for Isabella and Lucas' future. He revealed that Charles had been in contact with several intermediaries and was trying to build a case against them that could be used to pressure them.

"This is much more serious than we imagined," Hugo continued. "Charles is trying to use compromising information to force a resolution that favors his interests. The situation is delicate, and we need to act quickly to neutralize their influence."

Hugo's revelation brought a new dimension to the situation. Isabella and Lucas were now facing a direct threat that involved not only financial matters but also the possibility of a smear or blackmail campaign. The urgency of protecting your future and reputation has never been clearer.

With the help of Hugo, Robert Sinclair and the private investigator, Isabella and Lucas began to mount a strategic response. They devised a plan to expose Charles' intentions and gather all the evidence necessary to ensure he could not manipulate the situation to his advantage.

The following days were marked by frenetic activity. Isabella and Lucas worked with their team to consolidate the evidence and prepare a presentation that highlighted Charles' manipulations and intentions. The strategy involved a combination of legal action and public communication, with the aim of protecting their interests and ensuring they were not harmed.

Finally, the moment has arrived. Isabella and Lucas, accompanied by Robert and Hugo, arranged a meeting with Charles Wentworth to confront him with the evidence gathered and clarify the situation. The meeting was scheduled for a Tuesday afternoon, in a neutral location that offered privacy and security.

The meeting was tense from the beginning. Charles was aware that the situation was becoming more complicated and was prepared for a battle. He welcomed Isabella, Lucas, Robert and Hugo with a mixture of disdain and caution, knowing the pressure was mounting.

"So, you decided to gather all this evidence," Charles

commented, his voice thick with sarcasm. "What do you intend to do with this? Do you still think you can intimidate me?"

Isabella, with firm determination, presented the evidence and explained the situation. "Charles, we have information that clearly shows your attempts to manipulate the situation and exploit our vulnerabilities. We are not here to make threats, but to ensure that everything is resolved fairly and transparently."

Charles looked at the documents and the group, a look of frustration on his face. "Do you really believe you can take me down with this? I have resources and connections that go beyond what you imagine."

Tensions were at a fever pitch, and the meeting ended without a definitive resolution. Charles withdrew with a veiled threat of retaliation, leaving Isabella and Lucas feeling that the battle was far from over.

Chapter 14, **"Echoes of Destiny,"** explores the growing complexity of Isabella and Lucas' fight against Charles Wentworth. The new discoveries and Hugo Almeida's intervention add a layer of intrigue and urgency to the situation. The need for quick and strategic action, along with the pressure to protect their future and reputation, highlights the couple's strength and determination. The chapter illustrates the ongoing battle to face threats and manipulations, showing the importance of acting with caution and courage in the face of significant challenges.

CHAPTER 15: THE GAME OF TRUTH

The month of April arrived with a feeling of imminent tension for Isabella and Lucas. After the direct confrontation with Charles Wentworth, the atmosphere was charged with uncertainty and anxiety. Hugo Almeida's revelations and the private investigator's findings had put the situation in a new perspective, and the couple knew they needed to act with precision to ensure their safety and protect their future.

The days following the meeting with Charles were marked by a frenzy of activity. Isabella and Lucas were determined to face the challenge with a well-developed strategy. The support of Hugo Almeida and Robert Sinclair was instrumental in creating a robust approach that combined legal action and crisis management. The situation now required them to be meticulous and cautious, while Charles' pressure continued to be felt.

Lucas spent the morning reviewing the documents and evidence that had been gathered. He was determined not to miss any details and to ensure that all information was accurate and presentable. Isabella, in turn, was busy preparing a public statement that aimed to clarify the situation and protect her and Lucas's reputation.

Meanwhile, Robert Sinclair and Hugo Almeida worked in parallel to consolidate the evidence and prepare a presentation that would be used in a legal hearing scheduled for next week. The hearing was a crucial opportunity to expose Charles' intentions and ensure the truth was revealed.

On Thursday afternoon, Isabella and Lucas met with Hugo to discuss the final preparations. Hugo entered Isabella's office with a serious expression, carrying a folder full of documents and reports.

"We need to make sure everything is in order before the hearing," Hugo said, placing the folder on the table. "These are the investigator's final reports and legal documents that we will use to strengthen our position. Every detail is crucial."

Isabella and Lucas reviewed the documents carefully, reviewing each piece of evidence and ensuring everything was prepared for presentation. The work was intense and required total concentration, but the determination to protect his future helped him stay focused.

On the morning of the hearing, the courtroom was filled with tension. Isabella and Lucas arrived early, with the lawyers and the rest of the team, to prepare for the session. The atmosphere was formal, with the judge presiding over the case and an audience of observers and journalists present, eager to follow the proceedings.

Charles Wentworth arrived just before the hearing began, his presence providing an aura of confidence that contrasted with Isabella and Lucas's apprehension. He was accompanied by a team of lawyers who seemed equally prepared to face the challenge. The atmosphere was charged with anticipation and the anticipation was palpable.

The hearing began with the parties presenting their arguments. Robert Sinclair opened, giving an overview of the case and detailing the evidence that had been gathered. He highlighted Charles' manipulation and attempts to influence the situation for his own interests.

"Ladies and gentlemen of the jury," Robert began, his voice firm and clear. "We are here today to expose the truth about Charles Wentworth's actions and his attempt to manipulate the situation for his own benefit. The evidence we will present clearly demonstrates their questionable intentions and activities."

Lucas and Isabella listened attentively, feeling a mixture of relief and nervousness. The presentation of the evidence was a decisive moment, and they knew that every detail counted. Robert and the legal team were prepared to respond to any challenge or dispute that arose.

Charles' defense, led by an experienced and astute lawyer, began to argue against the evidence presented. They attempted to discredit the documents and argued that the evidence was insufficient to support the allegations. The defense lawyer also tried to create doubts about the integrity of the sources and the credibility of the documents.

During the hearing, Isabella and Lucas remained calm, although they were aware of the importance of every word and every argument. They focused on supporting Robert and his team, providing any additional information that might be needed to bolster their position.

After presenting the evidence and arguments from the parties involved, the judge closed the hearing and announced that the verdict would be released at a future date. Isabella and Lucas left the courtroom with a sense of relief mixed with anxiety. Waiting for the verdict was a new stage in the journey, and the final outcome was still pending.

In the days following the hearing, life continued at a frenetic pace. Isabella and Lucas met with Hugo and Robert to discuss the next steps and prepare for any eventuality. They were eager to receive the court's decision and hoped that justice would be served.

During this time, the couple also tried to find moments of calm and normality amidst the turmoil. They spent time together in activities they used to enjoy, like walks outside and quiet dinners, trying to find a sense of normalcy and balance.

Finally, the verdict date arrived. Isabella and Lucas addressed the court with a mixture of hope and apprehension. The atmosphere was charged with expectation, and the presence of Charles and his team of lawyers indicated that the final decision was about to be revealed.

The judge entered the room and announced the decision. The decision was in favor of Isabella and Lucas, and the allegations against Charles were substantially confirmed. The court had found sufficient evidence to support the charges and ensure that Charles' manipulation was properly addressed.

The decision brought significant relief to Isabella and Lucas. They were grateful to have overcome the challenge and to have the truth recognized. The victory in court not only protected their future, but also restored the sense of justice and integrity they sought.

Chapter 15, **"The Truth Game,"** explores the culmination of the confrontation between Isabella and Lucas and Charles Wentworth. The hearing and final decision represent a crucial point in the fight for justice and the protection of your interests. The chapter highlights the importance of meticulous preparation, determination, and courage in the face of challenges, and offers a meaningful conclusion to the battle the couple faced. The resolution of the case brings relief and a sense of accomplishment, reflecting the journey of overcoming and the search for truth in the midst of adversity.

CHAPTER 16: THE REFUGE OF TRUTH

With the court's decision in favor of Isabella and Lucas, the feeling of relief and justice brought a new perspective to the couple's lives. The verdict, which confirmed Charles Wentworth's manipulation and invalidated his attempts at exploitation, was a crucial milestone in their journey. However, although the weight of the accusations had been lifted, the need to rebuild and move forward was still a priority.

The day following the verdict was marked by a sense of calm and a renewed sense of hope. Isabella and Lucas met at the mansion, a space that, although it still carried traces of past tension, now felt like a place of recovery and renewal. The victory in court was just the beginning of a new phase, and the couple was determined to transform this experience into an opportunity to grow and strengthen their relationship.

Lucas, reflecting on the challenges they faced, began planning a series of changes and improvements to their lives and businesses. He was determined not to let the negative experience shape his future. Instead, I wanted to use the lessons learned to create a solid foundation for growth and prosperity.

Isabella, on the other hand, was focused on reevaluating her priorities and reestablishing her personal and professional goals. She knew that the fight against Charles had been a significant test, but now it was time to focus on her passions and projects that had been put on hold during the turmoil. He then decided to dedicate more time to social causes and promoting initiatives that contributed to the community.

The next morning, as the sun began to illuminate the mansion, Isabella and Lucas met in the garden to discuss their next steps. The surrounding environment was serene, with the vibrant greenery and the gentle sound of leaves blowing in the wind creating an ideal setting for meaningful conversation.

"Now that we have a fresh start," Lucas began, "I think it's time to think about how we can use this experience to create a positive impact. Not just in our businesses, but in our personal lives as well."

Isabella smiled and agreed. "I also feel like we need to redirect our energy towards something constructive. We have the opportunity to start again, and I want to take advantage of this to do something meaningful."

The couple discussed various ideas and possibilities, from charitable initiatives to new business projects. The decision to focus on social causes was especially important to Isabella, who had always felt a deep connection to promoting well-being and justice.

Within days, Isabella and Lucas began implementing their new initiatives. Isabella became involved in an organization that worked with vulnerable young people, offering guidance and support to help them achieve their goals. She also started her own project to promote female education and empowerment, reflecting her personal passions and values.

Lucas, in turn, focused on revitalizing his business and investing in new opportunities that aligned with his principles of integrity and innovation. He was determined to create a working environment that was both inspiring and ethical, using his experience to ensure his companies contributed positively to society.

While Isabella and Lucas were involved in their new projects, Hugo Almeida continued to be a constant presence in their lives. He had become a trusted friend and advisor, offering valuable support and guidance. Hugo was also involved in social impact initiatives and often collaborated with Isabella on her causes.

The friendship and mutual respect between Isabella, Lucas and Hugo deepened, and they began working together on various community projects. Initiatives included fundraising events, educational workshops and mentoring programs, all aimed at promoting well-being and personal development.

A significant event was the launch of a foundation created by Isabella and Lucas, with the aim of supporting and empowering people in vulnerable situations. The foundation focused on providing scholarships, job training, and emotional support to help individuals overcome challenges and achieve their goals.

The inauguration of the foundation was a remarkable and exciting moment. The event was attended by friends, family and collaborators, all gathered to celebrate the beginning of a new journey. Isabella and Lucas were greeted with enthusiasm and support, and the ceremony highlighted the positive impact the foundation would have on the community.

While the foundation began to make a difference, Isabella and Lucas also found time to relax and enjoy time together. They traveled to exotic destinations, explored new cultures, and spent quality time in activities that brought them joy and satisfaction.

The experience of facing challenges and overcoming adversity had strengthened Isabella and Lucas' relationship. They learned to value even more the importance of partnership, trust and mutual support. The period of recovery and renewal brought them closer together and helped them build a solid foundation for the future.

Isabella and Lucas's lives were now filled with new opportunities and challenges, but also with a deep sense of fulfillment and gratitude. They had turned a difficult situation into an opportunity to grow, positively impact the world around them, and build a meaningful legacy.

Chapter 16, **"The Haven of Truth,"** explores Isabella and Lucas' transition to a new phase in their lives after their court victory. The focus is on transforming adversity into opportunities for personal growth and social impact. The narrative highlights the importance of recovery, building a solid foundation, and getting involved in meaningful causes. The chapter celebrates the renewal and strengthening of the couple's relationship, illustrating how facing challenges can lead to a richer and more fulfilling life.

CHAPTER 17: THE REVELATION OF THE PAST

The month of May brought a renewed sense of tranquility and satisfaction for Isabella and Lucas. The foundation was thriving, and his personal and professional projects were expanding. However, an unexpected event was about to alter the trajectory of their lives once again.

On a Tuesday afternoon, while Isabella and Lucas were at the foundation office, a letter arrived, carefully addressed to Isabella. The envelope was simple, but there was something intriguing about it—there was no return address indicated, just Isabella's name in elegant letters. The sense of curiosity Isabella felt upon receiving the letter was palpable.

With the envelope in her hands, Isabella exchanged a look with Lucas. "I don't know what it is, but it seems important," she said, opening it carefully.

Inside was a handwritten letter, in fluid, elegant handwriting. Isabella began to read in a low voice:

"Dear Isabella,

I haven't heard from you in a long time, but the memories have never faded. I hope this letter finds you well and that you are living the full life you always deserved. There are secrets and truths from the past that need to be revealed. The time has come to clarify some issues that have been hidden for too long.

I'm your aunt, Maria Costa, and this is a revelation that could change everything you knew about your family and your past. Please contact me for a personal meeting. It will be an important conversation, and I would like to explain everything in detail.

With affection,

Maria Costa"

Isabella read the letter several times, trying to process the information. "My aunt... Maria Costa. I never knew I had an aunt with that name," she murmured, perplexed.

Lucas approached and looked at the letter. "Do you know this person? And why didn't she get in touch sooner?"

Isabella shook her head, confused. "I never heard of her. My parents never mentioned an aunt named Maria. This must have something to do with my family's past, something we don't know."

Determined to find out more about Isabella's mysterious aunt, the couple agreed to set up a meeting with Maria Costa. Within a few days, they met at an elegant café in the city center, where the welcoming atmosphere contrasted with the anxiety Isabella felt.

When Maria arrived, Isabella and Lucas were immediately captivated by her presence. She was a middle-aged woman with gray hair and an aura of dignity and grace. The expression on his face was a mix of seriousness and warmth, as if he carried the weight of many untold stories.

After the introductions and exchange of greetings, Maria sat with the couple at a private table. She took a deep breath before starting to speak.

"Isabella, Lucas, thank you for coming. I appreciate you giving me the opportunity to explain," Maria began, her voice soft and controlled. "I understand that this situation may be unexpected and upsetting, but there are things that need to be clarified."

She paused, watching Isabella's reaction. "I am your aunt on my mother's side, and many years ago, when you were still a child, your parents and I made decisions that altered the course of our lives. I had reasons to distance myself and keep certain information secret, but now I feel the time is right to speak out."

Isabella and Lucas listened intently, as Maria began to reveal secrets from the past that had been hidden for so long. She told of a series of events that had led to her estrangement from her family and the complications that arose.

"Your parents, Isabella, were involved in a very complicated business scheme," Maria explained. "They made some financial decisions that were hurtful, and to protect you and your siblings, I made the decision to step away and keep my distance. I knew this was painful, but it was a way to protect her safety and well-being."

Maria revealed that, in fact, Isabella's family's financial situation had been much more complex than it seemed. She described how a series of bad decisions and problematic investments had led to a financial collapse that was carefully covered up. Part of this cover-up involved removing Maria and hiding important information.

The revelation came as a shock to Isabella. "I never imagined our parents would be involved in something so complicated. Why didn't you tell us before?" she asked, her voice thick with emotion.

Maria sighed. "I understand your frustration, Isabella. At the time, I thought it was the best decision to protect you. I hoped that, with time, things could be resolved and that the truths could come to light in a less painful way. But now, I feel like it's time for you to know the full truth."

As Maria continued to explain the details, Isabella and Lucas were informed about a series of documents and records that had been kept secret. These documents detailed the financial transactions and agreements that had led to the problem, and Maria offered to share everything she knew.

The meeting with Maria left Isabella and Lucas with mixed feelings. The revelation brought a new understanding about the past, but it also opened up a series of questions and concerns about how to deal with the consequences of this truth.

After the meeting, Isabella and Lucas returned home feeling emotionally overwhelmed. The new perspective on Isabella and her family's past has left them with many thoughts about what to do next.

Lucas, concerned about the impact of the revelations, suggested they seek financial and legal advice to better understand the situation. Isabella agreed, recognizing the need to deal with the details in a careful and informed way.

In the following days, the couple worked with consultants and lawyers to review the documents and understand the implications of Maria's revelations. The situation was complex, but Isabella and Lucas were determined to face the challenges with transparency and resolution.

Chapter 17, **"The Revelation of the Past,"** explores the impact of unexpected revelations about Isabella's family and how they affect the couple's current lives. The narrative highlights the importance of truth and understanding the past to face future challenges. The revelation of family secrets and the need to deal with the financial and emotional consequences are central themes, illustrating how facing the truth can lead to new journeys and significant decisions.

CHAPTER 18: THE CHALLENGE OF TRUTH

The impact of the revelations about Isabella and Lucas' family past began to manifest itself in unexpected ways. Although the initial shock had been processed, the need to face reality brought to the surface a series of practical and emotional challenges. The next chapter of the story would be a journey of confrontation and reconstruction.

The day following the meeting with Maria Costa was marked by an atmosphere of tension and reflection. Isabella and Lucas were aware that they now had to deal with the consequences of the revelations. To do this, they decided to meet with a team of lawyers and financial consultants to better understand the situation and plan the next steps.

The law office was located in an elegant building in the city center. The environment, although professional, offered a feeling of welcome and seriousness. Isabella and Lucas entered the conference room, where they were greeted by a group of experts in law and finance.

The team's main lawyer, Dr. Eduardo Reis, greeted them with a firm handshake and a look of empathy. "Good morning, Isabella, Lucas. We are here to help you understand the situation and formulate a strategy to deal with the recent revelations."

After a brief introduction, Dr. Reis began to explain the details of the documents and records provided by Maria Costa. "The documents we received show a series of financial transactions and agreements that were made to protect the family's assets," the lawyer explained. "However, these actions have also resulted in several legal and financial issues that we need to address."

While Dr. Reis spoke, Isabella and Lucas reviewed the documents in front of them. The complexity of the information was impressive, and the need for clarification was evident. The lawyer highlighted several critical points, including the possible need to reverse some of the transactions and address financial compensation issues.

"The situation is delicate, but not insurmountable," continued Dr. Reis. "Our goal is to protect your interests and find the best way to resolve these issues fairly and effectively."

Isabella and Lucas listened intently, asking questions and discussing the implications of the revelations. The meeting lasted several hours, and at the end, the couple felt exhausted, but also more informed and prepared to face what was to come.

After meeting with the lawyers, Isabella and Lucas met with a team of financial advisors to get a more detailed look at the family's financial situation. The team presented a thorough analysis of the financials, highlighting areas that needed immediate attention and offering recommendations for restructuring.

Working with consultants revealed that Isabella's

family's financial situation was more complicated than it initially seemed. There were several outstanding issues, including debts to be paid off and assets that needed to be redistributed or sold. The restructuring process would be complex and would require a coordinated effort to ensure a balanced solution.

During the following weeks, Isabella and Lucas immersed themselves in the task of facing financial and legal issues. They worked with the team of lawyers and consultants to implement necessary changes and resolve outstanding issues. The work was intense and demanding, but the couple was determined to overcome the obstacles and restore financial stability.

While facing practical challenges, Isabella and Lucas also had to deal with emotional and personal issues. The revelation of the past had created a new dynamic in their lives, and the impact on family and personal relationships was profound.

Isabella began to dedicate more time to reflecting on her relationship with her family and the impact of the revelations on her relationships. She felt the need to reconnect with her siblings and explore how the changes would affect their family dynamics.

Lucas, for his part, was focused on ensuring the situation didn't negatively affect his relationship with Isabella. He offered ongoing support and understanding, recognizing that the journey was testing the strength of their relationship. Partnership and mutual commitment became even more important as they faced challenges together.

Amid the process of financial and emotional restructuring, Isabella and Lucas also found time to relax and support each other. They took time to escape their intense routine, traveling to peaceful destinations and enjoying activities that helped them recharge.

One of the most meaningful moments was a trip to a small seaside village, where Isabella and Lucas spent a few days in a serene retreat. The calm environment and natural beauty provided a much-needed pause to reflect on what they had achieved and the challenges they still faced.

During the trip, the couple had in-depth conversations about their hopes and plans for the future. They discussed how revelations about the past had changed their perspectives and how they were determined to move forward with renewed determination and purpose.

Upon returning from their trip, Isabella and Lucas found new energy to face the remaining challenges. The restructuring process was underway, and they were starting to see the results of the changes implemented.

The recovery of the family's financial situation was far from complete, but the couple felt they were on the right path. They had faced the revelations with courage and determination, and were now beginning to build a more solid and promising future.

Chapter 18, **"The Truth Challenge,"** explores the impact of the revelations on Isabella and Lucas' family and how they face the resulting financial and emotional challenges. The narrative highlights the importance of facing the truth and working together to overcome obstacles. The chapter illustrates the couple's journey in search of stability and recovery, showing how mutual support and determination can help face adversity and create a better future.

CHAPTER 19:
THE RETURN TO NORMALITY

Spring was advancing in its fullness, bringing with it an atmosphere of renewal and hope for Isabella and Lucas. After intense weeks of hard work to sort out the financial and legal complications, the couple was beginning to see a light at the end of the tunnel. The changes implemented were starting to take effect, and the feeling of relief was gradually replacing the stress.

The foundation office was back to its normal routine, with ongoing projects and events scheduled for the coming months. Isabella and Lucas were committed to ensuring that the foundation continued to thrive, even as they dealt with the personal challenges they had faced.

That morning, Isabella was reviewing financial reports when Lucas entered the office with a satisfied smile. "We have an important meeting with the foundation partners later, but I wanted to show you something," he said, handing Isabella an envelope.

She looked at the envelope curiously and opened it to find an invitation to a foundation gala. "It looks like the foundation is organizing a special event soon. This must be exciting," commented Isabella.

Lucas agreed. "Yes, and on top of that, we have some positive developments with ongoing projects. The new financial approach we have implemented is working well, and we are seeing significant improvements."

The gala promised to be a celebration of success and an opportunity for the foundation to showcase the results of its efforts. Isabella and Lucas were excited about the prospect of bringing together partners, supporters and community members to celebrate recent achievements.

As they prepared for the event, Isabella and Lucas took time to reflect on the journey they had taken. The transition from chaos to stability had not been easy, but they were grateful for the lessons learned and the strength of their relationship.

The night of the event arrived, and the elegant ballroom was stunning, decorated with elegance and sophistication. The guests were dressed in formal attire, and the atmosphere was one of celebration and enthusiasm. Isabella and Lucas welcomed their guests with smiles and warm greetings, feeling proud of what they had achieved.

During the event, Isabella gave a speech to thank the foundation's supporters and share recent successes. "We are immensely grateful for the support and trust you have shown," she began. "The challenges we faced were significant, but with the help of all of you, we were able to overcome them and reach new heights."

The speech was met with applause and praise, and

Isabella and Lucas felt renewed by the recognition and support of the community. The evening continued with a series of presentations and performances, creating an atmosphere of joy and celebration.

At the end of the event, as the guests said goodbye and the foundation team began to dismantle the decorations, Isabella and Lucas found a moment to reflect on the importance of what they had achieved. The celebration was not only a mark of success, but also a symbol of the strength and resilience they had shown in facing challenges.

In the following days, the couple continued to focus on the foundation and future projects. The recent experience had reinforced his commitment to the organization's mission and creating a positive impact in the community. They were excited about the opportunities that lay ahead and determined to continue to build on the success they had achieved.

As spring progressed, Isabella and Lucas found time to relax and enjoy personal time. They planned a short trip to a destination they had always wanted to visit, a welcome break to celebrate their achievements and strengthen their relationship.

The trip provided a refreshing escape from routine and an opportunity for Isabella and Lucas to reconnect. They explored new places, enjoyed delicious meals, and spent quiet time together, away from the pressures and responsibilities of everyday life.

During the trip, the couple had in-depth conversations about their dreams and aspirations for the future. They discussed how the recent experience had changed their perspectives and how they were looking forward to continuing to build a future together.

Upon returning from the trip, Isabella and Lucas felt

renewed and ready to face the next challenges. The foundation was on a solid path, and they were committed to continuing to make a difference. The chapter of the financial crisis was closing, and a new chapter of growth and success was opening.

Chapter 19, **"The Return to Normality,"** explores Isabella and Lucas' transition into a new phase of their lives after facing significant challenges. The narrative highlights the importance of celebrating achievements and finding balance between responsibilities and personal moments. The chapter illustrates the couple's recovery and growth, showing how the strength of their relationship and dedication to work can lead to a promising and rewarding future.

FINAL CONSIDERATIONS

As we approach the end of "The Lovers of Luxury: Passion and Prejudice," we are invited to reflect on the profound emotional journey and complexities that defined Isabella and Lucas' path. This novel is not just a love story, but a modern epic that explores universal themes of passion, pride, and the impact of past choices on the present and future.

The plot, rich in details and nuances, presents us with a vivid portrait of how appearances can be deceptive and how hidden truths can come to light, challenging perceptions and altering destinies. Isabella and Lucas, through their tumultuous and transformative experiences, exemplify the struggle between the desire to maintain an idealized image and the need to face raw reality. Her journey is a powerful illustration of how love and commitment can be tested and strengthened in the face of adversity.

Throughout the chapters, we follow the evolution of the characters as they face personal and professional challenges.

The revelation of family secrets and financial difficulties represent just one part of the complex puzzle that each person must solve. The way Isabella and Lucas deal with these adversities not only shapes their own future, but also reflects on the importance of truth, resilience and trust in a relationship.

Moments of tension and drama are interspersed with periods of celebration and fulfillment, showing that, despite difficulties, there is always room for hope and recovery. The foundation's gala symbolizes the triumph over difficulties and the reaffirmation of the values and objectives that define the identity of the protagonists. Isabella and Lucas' journey is a testament to the strength of partnership and the power of mutual support, essential to overcoming obstacles and building a lasting legacy.

Furthermore, the novel offers a subtle and sophisticated critique of the social and cultural dynamics that influence our lives and choices. The struggle between maintaining a status quo and seeking authenticity is a central theme, reflecting the reality of many readers who can identify with the complexities presented.

The final considerations serve as a reminder that although challenges are inevitable, how we choose to face them defines our trajectory. Isabella and Lucas show us that, with courage, commitment and genuine love, it is possible to transform adversities into opportunities and create a future full of possibilities.

Ultimately, "The Lovers of Luxury: Passion and Prejudice" invites us to celebrate not only the triumphs, but also the lessons learned along the way. The story of Isabella and Lucas is an ode to the strength of the human spirit and the ability to find beauty and meaning even in the most difficult times. May this narrative continue to inspire and move, reflecting the universality of feelings and the importance of facing life with an open heart and resilient mind.

www.ingramcontent.com/pod-product-compliance
Lightning Source LLC
Chambersburg PA
CBHW061504250726

48657CB00005B/1723